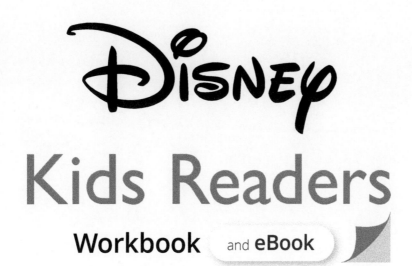

Disney

Kids Readers

Workbook and **eBook**

Level

5

Sandy Zerva and Kathryn Harper

P Pearson

Contents

Book 1

How does Bo Peep feel? What do
you see that makes you say that?
Think and talk.

Vocabulary

1 Label the pictures.

figure ....

  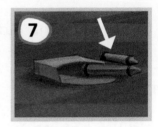 

....

2 Match the pairs.

1 antique   **2** far   **3** kindergarten   **4** lost   **5** worried

a happy   **b** new   **c** found   **d** college   **e** near

3 Sort the words.

~~crayon~~ GPS carousel crash motorbike
backpack carnival kindergarten RV glue

Fun
....
....

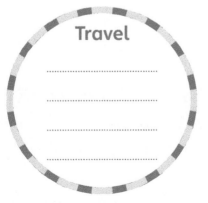

Travel
....
....
....
....

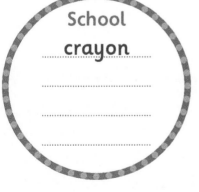

School
crayon
....
....
....

Story

1 Complete the main ideas. There is one extra phrase.

> is different   do what is good for others   can be good   lose hope

1 Gabby Gabby was sad because she didn't have a kid. In the end she found one.

Main idea: Don't ....

2 Bo didn't want to be with one kid, like other toys. She wanted to be free.

Main idea: Everyone .... and that's okay.

3 Woody left his old life behind to begin a new life with Bo.

Main idea: Change ....

2 How does Woody feel? Why?

| 1 | 10 | 12 | 28 |

| He feels | .... | .... | .... |
| because Bonnie | .... | .... | .... |

3 ✏️ At the end of the story, Woody said goodbye to his friends to start a new life with Bo. Do you think he did the right thing? Why or why not? Write in your notebook.

I think he didn't do the right thing because ...

4

Language

1 🎧 **Listen and read.**

2 **Look at Lila's planner. Write what she is and isn't doing.**

FRI	SAT	SUN	MON
~~tennis~~ visit Grandma	watch soccer with Dad	bake cookies with Mom and Finn	~~go to movies~~ cousins come!

1 On Friday, Lila <u>isn't playing tennis</u>. She <u>'s visiting her grandma</u>.

2 On Saturday, Lila and her dad ....

3 On Sunday, they ....

4 On Monday, ...

3 **Write the verb in the present progressive or the present simple.**

1 Ollie: What .... (do) this weekend?

2 Jenna: We .... (have) a sushi night on Saturday. Mom usually .... (buy) sushi from the store, but this time my dad .... (make) them.

3 Ollie: Nice! I .... (go) to Lucy's party on Sunday.

4 Jenna: Me, too! I always .... (give) her a book for her birthday, but this time she .... (get) a surprise!

4 **Write your plans for the weekend. Then play a guessing game.**

On Saturday morning, you're doing your homework.

No, I'm not. I'm playing baseball.

Phonics

1 🎧 **Read and underline oi or oy. Then match three sentences to the pictures. Listen and check.**

1 This boy has a toy.
2 What a nice voice!
3 Joy points at her toy.
4 Count your coins.
5 Too much noise!
6 The girls join hands.

2 🎧 **Write the missing words with oi and oy. Then listen and say.**

A long time ago, when I was a b_____
There were a lot of t_____ for me to en_____ .
But my favorite of all my t_____
Was one for keeping all my c_____ .

A long time ago, when I was a girl
My favorite t_____ in all the world
Was not a doll with a lovely v_____ .
It was a t_____ for making a lot of n_____ !

3 🎧 **Listen and spell words with oi and oy. Find the secret word and complete the sentence.**

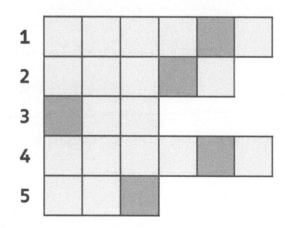

They're going to _____ their life together.

Global Citizenship

1 Read and circle **T (True)** or **F (False)**. In pairs, correct the false sentences.

1 Some pet owners can't or don't want to take care of their pets. **T / F**

2 *Battersea Dogs and Cats Home* is in every city in England. **T / F**

3 The *Battersea Dogs and Cats Home* takes care of more than six thousand animals a year. **T / F**

4 If you're looking for a new pet, you can look at the animals on the Internet. **T / F**

2 Why do pets lose their homes? Write one reason for each animal. Use the ideas in the box or your own.

noisy   dirty   expensive   sick   run/fly away

Bird
....
....

Cat
....
....

Dog
....
....

Mouse
....
....

3 Taking care of a pet is a big responsibility. In pairs, think of a possible problem with having a pet and a solution.

> I have a dog, but I want to go away on vacation. I can't take it with me.

> You could ask a family member to look after your dog. Make sure they have enough time to do it!

Find Out

1 **Write the numbers. In groups, talk about the information. How does it make you feel?**

> 1   2016   365   1,000,000   450

1   The information about plastic bottles is from the year ....

2   In that year, people bought .... plastic drink bottles every minute.

3   Plastic bottles take .... years to break into smaller parts.

4   Bea Johnson's family only filled .... jar with trash in a whole year.

2 **How can you use less plastic every day?**

Writing tip

People often use plastic things once, then throw them away.

> Use *then* to show the order of two actions.

3 **In your notebook, join sentences 1–4 using *then*. Complete sentences 5–6 with your own ideas.**

1   People buy plastic water bottles. People throw away the plastic bottles.

2   The plastic bottles decompose. The plastic bottles become microplastics.

3   Fish eat the microplastics. Fish die.

4   We don't take action. The pollution becomes worse.

5   We drink water from metal bottles,

6   We don't buy single-use plastic,

Game Follow the Path

Start

1 Why is Bonnie worried at the beginning of the story?

2 What happened before and after this picture?

3 Who does Woody meet at the antique store?

7 How is Woody different from Bo Peep? Give two examples.

6 Say and spell it.

You play with this and it rhymes with *boy*.

5 What happens to old plastic when it goes into the ocean?

4 Use *then* to join sentences.

Forky climbed to an open window. Forky jumped out the window.

8 You fall in the trash! Lose a turn.

9 How much waste did Bea Johnson's family make for one whole year?

10 What does Duke Caboom do twice?

13 You're stuck in the cupboard! Lose a turn.

12 What are you doing this weekend? Say two sentences.

11 Why do pets go to an animal home? Give one reason.

14 Say and spell it.

This word rhymes with *choice* and you use it to speak or sing.

15 Name one old friend and one new friend Woody makes in the story.

16 What are Woody and Bo-Peep doing next?

Finish

Now I can...

◯ understand a story about toys.

◯ talk about definite plans using the present progressive tense.

◯ read, spell, and say words with oi and oy.

Disney ALICE IN WONDERLAND

Where is Alice? How does this
picture make you feel? Think and talk.

Vocabulary

1 **Do the crossword.**

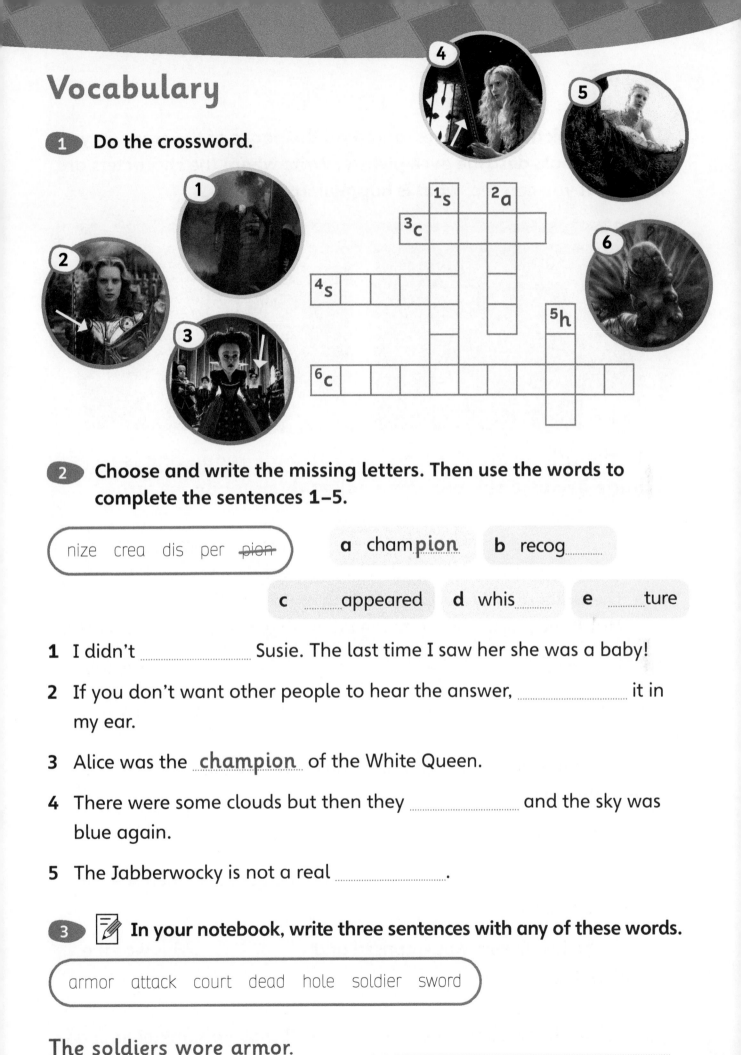

2 **Choose and write the missing letters. Then use the words to complete the sentences 1–5.**

nize   crea   dis   per   ~~pion~~

a cham**pion**   **b** recog............

c ....appeared   **d** whis............   **e** ....ture

1 I didn't .... Susie. The last time I saw her she was a baby!

2 If you don't want other people to hear the answer, ... it in my ear.

3 Alice was the ...champion... of the White Queen.

4 There were some clouds but then they .... and the sky was blue again.

5 The Jabberwocky is not a real ....

3 ✒️ **In your notebook, write three sentences with any of these words.**

armor   attack   court   dead   hole   soldier   sword

The soldiers wore armor.

Story

1 ✏️ **Look at the pictures, and read the pages of the story. In your notebook, describe each picture. Write where the characters are, what you can see, what is happening, and why.**

1

`5` `6`

2

`12` `13`

In the first picture, Alice is in a strange room. She is huge because she ate some cake which made her grow big. In her hand, she is holding ...

2 **The writer uses interesting words to make the story more exciting. Match the pairs. Then write the interesting words in the sentences.**

.... very good .... scared .... very big .... very bad

a terrible **b** huge **c** wonderful **d** frightened

1 `6` She ate some cake, and now she grew very tall. "Wonderful!" Alice thought.

2 `11` The Red Queen had a .... head.

3 `21` Alice felt .... She ran into the gardens. Then she sat down and cried.

4 `25` The Red Queen was surprised and .... This was the end for her.

3 ✏️ **At the end of the story, Alice says: "I shall do something good with my life." What do you think she did? Write in your notebook.**

Language

1 🎧 **Listen and read.**

2 **Complete with *could* + verb. Write AS = asking for a suggestion, S = making a suggestion, or R = making a request.**

Ben: What ___could I do___ (I / do) with my old tablet? ....

Dad: _____ (you / give) it to Grandma. ....

_____ (she / use) it to find recipes. ....

Ben: Good idea! _____ (Mom / take) it to her? ....

Dad: She's busy. _____ (we / take) it to her. ....

3 **Make a suggestion or request. Use *could*.**

1   (borrow)?   I'm sorry, I'm using my pen at the moment.

2   What could we do with all these apples?   (apple pie)

3   (homework)?   Sorry, I'm busy. You could ask Tim to help.

4   What could they do this weekend?   (skating)

4 **Plan a surprise party for a friend's birthday. Talk about decorations, the birthday cake, food, drink and music.**

 What could we do for Meg's birthday party?

We could make her a birthday cake.

13

Phonics

1 🎧 **Read and underline ou and ow. Then draw. Listen and check.**

1 A round owl sits on a cloud.

2 A brown cow flies over the town.

2 🎧 **Write the missing words with ou and ow. Then listen and say.**

The Mad Hatter's hat was b_____ and r_____.
When the Hatter went _____t, it fell on the g_____.

Without a s_____, that hat went d_____.
Then the D_____ found it, on the g_____.

"How did it fall?" the D_____ said,
But the Hatter was _____t, so she went to bed.

3 🎧 **Look and spell words with ou and ow. Which two words are the odd ones out? Listen and check.**

1 **a**   **b**   **c**

....

2 **a**   **b**   **c**

....

Global Citizenship

1 Read and circle T (True) or F (False). In pairs, talk about sentence 4.

1 Haile's family got sad when her dad got sick.   **T / F**

2 Haile's family changed their habits and became healthier. **T / F**

3 Haile's dad got better because a doctor helped him.   **T / F**

4 Good health can make you happier.   **T / F**

2 How healthy are these things? Complete the chart. Then talk about how habits can be healthier.

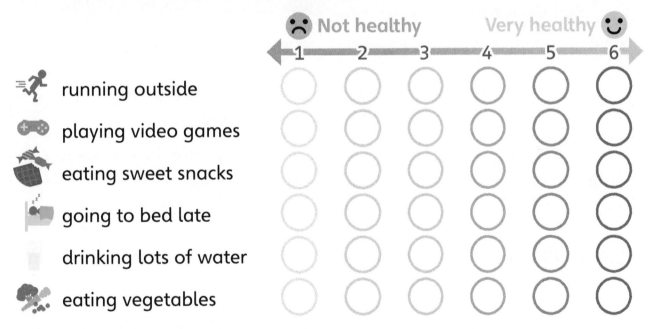

☹ Not healthy   Very healthy ☺

1 — 2 — 3 — 4 — 5 — 6

running outside ○ ○ ○ ○ ○ ○

playing video games ○ ○ ○ ○ ○ ○

eating sweet snacks ○ ○ ○ ○ ○ ○

going to bed late ○ ○ ○ ○ ○ ○

drinking lots of water ○ ○ ○ ○ ○ ○

eating vegetables ○ ○ ○ ○ ○ ○

3 In pairs, choose a problem and discuss how you can help.

Your little brother won't eat vegetables.

Your dad sits at his desk all day and doesn't move.

A friend is always tired in class.

I know! We could make an exercise plan for Dad.

Yes, and we could exercise with him every day.

15

Find Out

1 Complete the sentences about the Red Queen's makeup and clothes.

1 She is wearing a big, red wig on her ....

2 Her .... is very high.

3 She has very thin ....

4 There is a red heart on her ....

5 Her .... is red and gold. There are gold hearts on it.

2 🔆 Choose another character from the story. What does their "look" tell you about them? How are they different than the Red Queen?

Writing tip

First, **draw pictures of her.** *Then,* **make a wig.**
Finally, **design her clothes.**

Use linking words *first, then,* and *finally,* to order instructions.
Add a comma after the linking word.

3 Look at the notes and write the instructions in order. Use linking words and punctuation.

Costume
sew the costume
draw the costume
cut the material
find the material

.... First, ... draw ..... the costume. .....

.... the material

....

.... sew ....

Wig
make the wig
draw some ideas
prepare the material
measure the head

....

....

....

....

Game Pair Quiz

Student A

1a What's the odd one out?

armor sword hole battle

2a What blue creature does Alice meet?

3a Spell it.
The Mad Hatter's hat is br........n and r........nd.

4a Say two words to describe the character of the Red Queen.

5a Why does the Red Queen wear a lot of red?

6a Your friend can't open the door. Make a suggestion with *could*.

7a Why did Haile Thomas's family change the way they lived?

8a Make a question and ask your partner.

Student B

1b What's the odd one out?

creature court caterpillar rabbit

2b How did Alice get through the door?

3b Spell it.
The m........se lives in the h........se.

4b Say two words to describe the character of the White Queen.

5b How did the filmmakers make the Red Queen's head look bigger?

6b You want to join a game. Make a request with *could*.

7b What things can young people do with the HAPPY organization? Name two.

8b Make a question and ask your partner.

Now I can ...

○ understand a story about a fantastic place full of strange creatures.

○ make suggestions and requests with *could*.

○ read, spell, and say words with ou and ow.

Book 3

Disney · Pixar
WALL·E

What things in the picture are from the future? How do you know this is in space? Think and talk.

Vocabulary

1 ▸ **Read, then do the word search.**

1 to break up in little pieces

2 to leave the ground and start flying

3 to use a machine to see what's inside something

4 to run away from danger

5 to push something into a flatter shape

6 to do something without being afraid

e	b	w	e	q	v	l	h	t
x	f	r	d	k	g	b	b	a
p	s	q	u	a	s	h	r	k
l	f	o	d	e	s	y	a	e
o	t	c	j	p	c	g	v	o
d	a	e	s	c	a	p	e	f
e	n	z	u	c	n	h	l	f
s	i	j	a	m	x	i	y	k

2 ▸ **What do these groups of words have in common? Choose and write.**

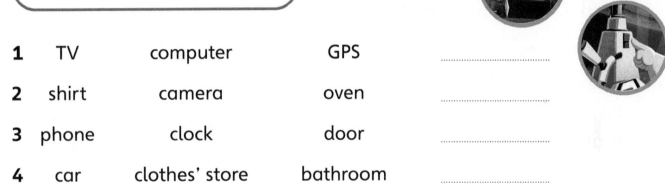

> alarm   screen   mirror   buttons

1   TV   computer   GPS   ....

2   shirt   camera   oven   ....

3   phone   clock   door   ....

4   car   clothes' store   bathroom   ....

3 ▸ **In pairs, do the quiz.**

1 What is the opposite of *appear*? ....

2 What goes down a chute? ....

3 What do you do to something that is broken? ....

4 What does a fire extinguisher do? ....

5 What's the opposite of *take off*? ....

6 What does a detector do? ....

Story

1 Read and circle T (True) or F (False). How do you know? Find clues in the story.

1 | 2 | At the beginning of the story, WALL-E feels lonely.   **T / F**

....

2 | 3 | 8 | For WALL-E, the plant is just a small, green thing.   **T / F**

....

3 | 11 | 19 | 21 | WALL-E is brave.   **T / F**

....

4 | 15 | 24 | 26 | Robots always do what people tell them.   **T / F**

....

2 | 1 | **Imagine you are on Earth with WALL-E at the beginning of the story. Complete the sentences.**

I can see ....

I can smell ....

I can hear ....

I can feel ....

3 At the end of the story, people return to Earth. What do you think their life will be like? How can they make it a beautiful place to live in again? Write in your notebook.

20

Language

1 🎧 **Listen and read.**

> ## 💬 Language
>
> Can you see **any**thing in the sky? Yes, I can see **some**thing.
> There are stars **every**where, but the moon is **no**where tonight.
> Use *some-*, *any-*, *no-*, *every-* + ***thing*** / ***where*** to describe things or places without saying exactly what or where they are.

2 **Complete with *some-*, *any-*, *no-*, *every-*.**

1 The big bowl fell and broke. Now there's glass .... where.

2 There isn't .... where to park the car.

3 I don't need .... thing. I have .... thing I need with me.

4 There's .... thing in the box. What is it?

3 **Complete the dialog. Use *some-*, *any-*, *no-*, *every-* + *thing/where*.**

Mark: I'm looking ...., but I can't find my phone.

Gina: There's .... on the shelf. Is that it?

Mark: No, that's a tablet.

Gina: Did you go .... with it today?

Mark: No, I didn't. It's .... in the house.

4 **Play a game. Make sentences with *some-*, *any-*, *no-*, *every-* + *thing/where*. Use the pictures or your own ideas.**

 Make a sentence with *somewhere*.

There's a burger restaurant somewhere near here.

Phonics

1 🎧 Help WALL-E find EVE. Read and follow the words with a soft g sound as in *large*. Listen and check.

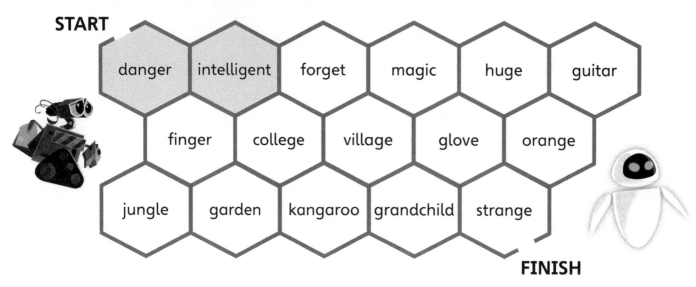

START

danger | intelligent | forget | magic | huge | guitar

finger | college | village | glove | orange

jungle | garden | kangaroo | grandchild | strange

FINISH

2 🎧 Write the missing words with a soft g sound. Then listen and say.

The l_____ captain
Looks in the f_____.
He's feeling very hungry.

He sees a ch_____.
No food? That's s_____!
And now he's feeling angry.

3 🎧 Listen and write the missing words. Underline words with a soft g sound.

1 A _____ _____.

2 A _____ in a _____.

3 _____ are _____!

4 The _____ is black and _____.

Global Citizenship

1 **Answer the questions. Write notes.**

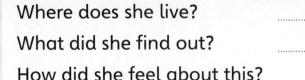

Profile of Autumn Peltier

Where does she live?   ....

What did she find out?   ....

How did she feel about this?   ....

What does she believe?   ....

What did she do?   ....

2 **What happens when we use clean or dirty water? Sort the sentences. Then talk with your partner. Add more ideas if you can.**

1 If you drink this, you can get sick.

2 We can use this to wash our clothes.

3 We can use this to take a shower.

4 This can hurt our skin.

5 We can't clean our houses with this.

6 If you drink this, you stay healthy.

✔
clean water
◯ ◯ ◯

✗
dirty water
◯ ◯ ◯

3 🔆 **Autumn helped people in her community. What is a problem in your community? How can you help? In small groups, think of three ways.**

Problem: ....

There's a lot of trash on the beach and in the water.

We could do a beach clean-up.

Find Out

1 Write one word to complete each sentence. Check the things you did *not* know.

> **1** The ISS goes around the world in 90 _____ . ◯
>
> **2** Many people think that the Sun is a _____ . That's not true, it's a star. ◯
>
> **3** The _____ planet is Jupiter. ◯
>
> **4** Venus isn't cold. In fact, it's the _____ planet. ◯

2 🔆 Could you be an astronaut? What is exciting or frightening about space travel?

📋 Writing tip

There are millions of pieces of trash in space.

Use uncountable nouns with phrases such as *a piece of* or *a box of*.

3 Choose and write. Use these phrases.

> a part of   a piece of   a drop of   a bit of   a box of

1 _____ space trash can travel fast and damage space stations.

2 _____ rain usually takes two minutes to reach the ground.

3 Earth, our planet, is _____ of space.

4 The astronauts took _____ soil to grow plants in space.

5 The scientists studied _____ moon dust under their microscopes.

Game Connect Four in a Line

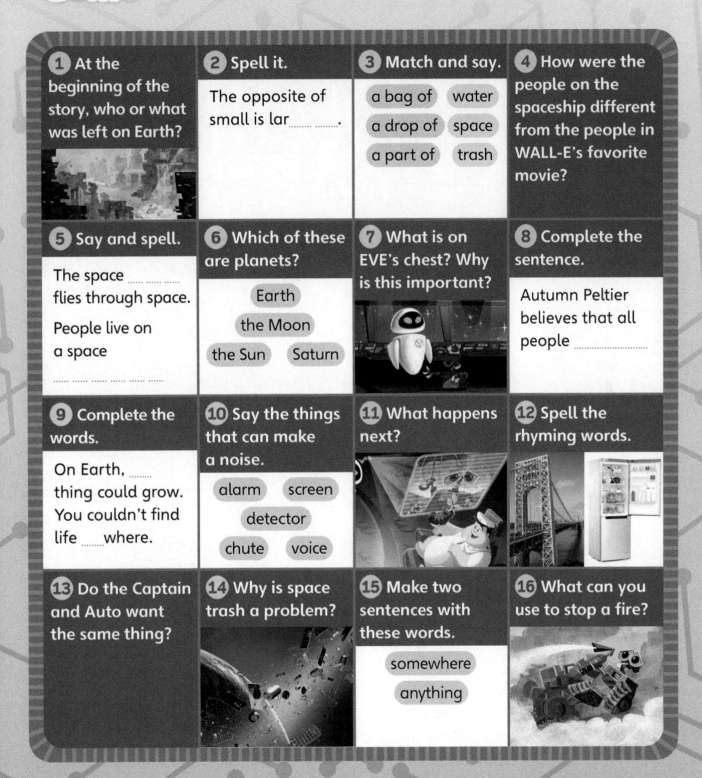

1 At the beginning of the story, who or what was left on Earth?

2 Spell it.

The opposite of small is lar........ ....

3 Match and say.

a bag of — water
a drop of — space
a part of — trash

4 How were the people on the spaceship different from the people in WALL-E's favorite movie?

5 Say and spell.

The space ....
flies through space.

People live on a space
....

6 Which of these are planets?

Earth
the Moon
the Sun   Saturn

7 What is on EVE's chest? Why is this important?

8 Complete the sentence.

Autumn Peltier believes that all people ....

9 Complete the words.

On Earth, ... thing could grow. You couldn't find life .... where.

10 Say the things that can make a noise.

alarm   screen
detector
chute   voice

11 What happens next?

12 Spell the rhyming words.

13 Do the Captain and Auto want the same thing?

14 Why is space trash a problem?

15 Make two sentences with these words.

somewhere
anything

16 What can you use to stop a fire?

Now I can...

○ understand a story about robots and space.

○ describe things or places without saying exactly what or where they are.

○ read, spell, and say words with a soft g sound.

Disney
Beauty
AND THE
Beast

Where is Belle? What is the mood
of this picture? Think and talk.

Vocabulary

1 Match the words that have a similar meaning.

1 crazy   **2** escape   **3** frighten   **4** staff   **5** spell

a run away   **b** magic   **c** workers   **d** scare   **e** mad

2 Choose a verb. Then find examples of these phrases in the story.

look   dream   return   live   lock   put

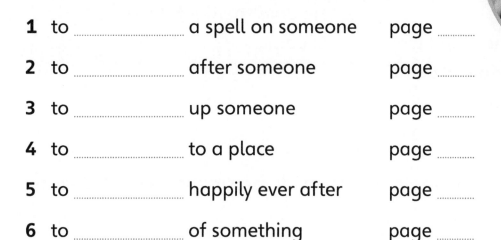

1 to .... a spell on someone   page ....

2 to .... after someone   page ....

3 to .... up someone   page ....

4 to .... to a place   page ....

5 to .... happily ever after   page ....

6 to .... of something   page ....

3 Sort the words. Draw a star next to the things that were enchanted in the story.

teapot   horse   forest   mirror   rose   music box   wolf   candlestick
teacup   petal

Plants

Things in the house

Animals

Story

1 Compare Beauty and the Beast. Find their differences and similarities.

Beauty	The Beast
1 Her father loves her.	....
2	He loves reading.
3 She is kind. Example: She bought bread for the old woman.	At the beginning, ... Example: ....
4 .... Example: She didn't leave the Beast to die after he fought the wolves.	He does the right thing. Example: ....

2 Complete the fairy tale fact file with information from the story.

Fairytale   Beauty and the Beast

Beginning: Once upon a time, a handsome prince lived in a castle.

End: Belle and the prince lived ....

Time: Sometime in the ....

Settings: A village, ...

Characters: Good: ....
          Bad: ....

Magical characters/objects: ....

3 What is your favorite scene in the story? Why? Write about it in your notebook.

Language

1 🎧 **Listen and read.**

💬 Language

If we look after plants, they stay healthy.
If we don't water them, they die.
Use **If + present tense** to talk about things that are always true, or habits. Add a comma between the clauses.

2 **Match 1–4 to a–d.**

> If I'm late for school, I ask my mom to drive me.

1 If I finish my homework early, ...   **a** I always give them a card.

2 If the next day is a holiday, ...   **b** I always go to bed early.

3 If I have school the next day, ...   **c** I play with my sister.

4 If it's a friend's birthday, ...   **d** I usually go to bed late.

3 **Write. Finish the sentences about things that people usually do in these situations.**

1 If it's warm, <u>we wear light clothes</u>.

2 If it's dark, ...

3 If it rains, ...

4 If it's hot, ...

4 **Say what is true for you. Then play a guessing game.**

> If I'm excited / bored / hungry / sad ...

> If Oscar's excited, he screams.

> No, if I'm excited, I talk a lot.

29

Phonics

1 🎧 **Listen and count the number of syllables. Then sort the words.**

1 soccer   **3** remember   **5** player   **7** armor

2 visitor   **4** river   **6** butter   **8** detector

Two syllables	Three syllables
soccer,	visitor,

2 🎧 **Write the missing words with er or or. Then listen and say.**

I'll use the m_____ to show me Belle.
Is she the one to break the spell?

Her love could end these years of w_____,
And give me back the c_____ of s_____.

Can she love me—the Beast in the t_____,
Before the last petal falls from the f_____?

3 🎧 **Listen and spell words with er and or. Find the secret word. Where are Belle and the Prince going tonight?**

```
    1 □ □ ■ □ □
    2 □ □ □ ■ □ □ □
    3 □ □ □ ■ □ □
    4 ■ □ □ □ □
    5 □ □ □ ■ □ □ □
    6 □ □ ■ □ □ □ ■
    7 □ □ □ □ □ ■ □
```

They're going to the _____

Global Citizenship

1 Put Malala's story into the correct order.

○ Malala grew up in the Swat Valley, Pakistan.

○ The Taliban closed the girls' schools.

○ Malala told the newspapers about the Taliban.

○ The Taliban attacked and hurt Malala.

○ Malala went to school.

○ Malala went to a hospital in England.

○ Malala fights for girls' schools all over the world.

2 What do you think about school? Check (✔) if you agree. Cross (✗) if you disagree. Then talk with your partner.

1 All girls have to learn to read. ○

2 Only girls must go to school. ○

3 School is bad for girls. ○

4 Reading is important for girls and boys. ○

5 Boys and girls can learn at home. ○

abc

3 How does reading help us? Ask and answer with your partner. How many answers can you find in two minutes?

How does reading help us?

Reading helps us understand signs.

Find Out

1 **What is true about fairy tales? Read and circle
T (True) or F (False).**

1 All fairy tales are less than fifty years old.   T / F

2 The first written fairy tale came from China.   T / F

3 Hans Christian Andersen wrote the Snow Queen.   T / F

4 The most popular animal in fairy tales is the frog.   T / F

5 The Brothers Grimm wrote fairy tales for children.   T / F

2  **Talk about your favorite fairy tale. What lesson does
it teach us?**

Writing tip

*Little Red Riding Hood is a fairy tale about a young girl
and a big, bad wolf.*

Use adjectives to add detail to sentences.

3 **Read the introduction to this fairy tale. Add the adjectives.**

clever   delicious   famous   large   sick   young

In this .... story, Little Red Riding
Hood is walking through the forest to visit
her .... grandmother. She meets
a .... wolf on the path. He wants
to eat the .... girl, her basket of
.... food, and Grandma, too! So,
the .... wolf makes a plan …

Game Follow the Path

Start

1 Join the sentences with *If*.

Children read books.
They do better at school.

2 What three things come to life in the story?

3 Why was Hans Christian Andersen unhappy when he was a boy? Give two reasons.

7 What prize did Malala win?

6 Why is the rose important in the story? Give two reasons.

5 You're in the prison in the castle! Miss a turn.

4 Who put a spell on the Beast? Why?

8 Spell it!

9 Use two adjectives to describe Belle.

10 What words go together?

petal	cup
teapot	key
lock	rose

13 What two characters change into other things?

12 You're stuck in the tavern with Gaston! Miss a turn.

11 What happens if girls don't go to school? Use *If*.

14 What two mistakes does Maurice make?

15 Spell it!

16 What lesson does the Beauty and the Beast teach us?

Finish

Now I can...

○ understand a story about a magic spell.

○ talk about things that are always true or habits using *if* + present tense.

○ read, spell, and say words with er and or.

What is happening in this picture?
How do the colors make you feel?
Think and talk.

Vocabulary

1 Cross out the incorrect spelling. Then match the words (1–8) to the images (a–h).

1 ~~lup~~ / lab a

2 cracs / crash ....

3 smoge / smoke ....

4 explosion / explusion ....

5 armar / armor ....

6 portal / portol ....

7 video / vidio ....

8 controls / controlls ....

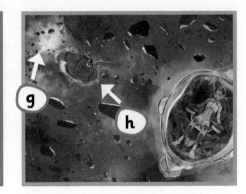

2 Find words in the story that are related to *computer*. Add them to the chart.

screen — computer

3 ✏️ In your notebook, write three sentences with any of these words. You can use any verb tense or make the nouns plural.

attack   control   destroy   mask   mind   safe

<u>The robot controlled his mind.</u>

Story

1 Answer the questions about details of the story.

1 Where did Tadashi work?

....

2 How did Hiro control the Microbots?

....

3 Who did Tadashi try to save?

....

4 What did the red chip do?

....

5 What stopped Baymax from fighting?

....

2 Match the pictures with the sound words. Then explain what they mean in the story.

1 [1] SCREECH! _c_   The motorbike stopped suddenly.

2 [4] Ouuuuch! ....

3 [7] KABOOOOM! ....

4 [13] BEEP! ....

5 [25] Whooosh! ....

3 📝 Imagine you can re-write page 7 of the story. What changes do you want to make? Write in your notebook.

Language

1 🎧 **Listen and read.**

2 **Imagine the future. Write. Use the correct form of *will* + verb.**

1 👧 Tanisha: ___Will___ we ___live___ (live) in big cities?

👧 Kat: Yes, _____. We _____ (live) in very tall

buildings. There _____ (be) gardens at the top.

2 👦 Dean: _____ people _____ (travel) in cars?

👧 Abby: No, _____. They _____ (use) flying pods.

There _____ (not be) any cars in the street.

3 **What will robots do in the future? Make predictions using the photos and your own ideas.**

4 **In pairs, imagine what your life will be like 30 years from now.**

I'll live in a very tall building, on the 300th floor.

How will you go up there?

I'll fly up in my car. Then I'll park it on the balcony.

Phonics

1 🎧 **Read and circle the letters for the sounds f and n. Listen and check.**

1 Fred wears headphones and Daphne has a microphone.

2 Noah ties a knot on the doorknob and knocks on the door.

2 🎧 **Write the missing words with ph and kn. Then listen and say.**

Hiro saw a d_____ in the San Fransokyo Bay.
He quickly took a _____ to before it swam away.

Then someone _____ed his hand, and his _____ne fell
on the floor.
Was his _____ne destroyed? He didn't _____ow for
sure.

He got down on his _____es – _____ew! His
_____ne was okay.
And the _____to of the d_____ was the best one
of the day!

3 🎧 **Listen and write ph or f, and kn or n. Then match 1–4 to a–d.**

1 Al____red the ele____ant has a ____riend.

2 The ____ight ____ows how to ____it a sweater.

3 So____ie came ____irst and won the tro____y.

4 ____ick cut the ____ot with his ____ife.

a

b

c

d

Global Citizenship

1 Circle the correct words.

1 It's hard to find **green spaces / empty rooftops** in big cities.

2 Rooftop Republic builds gardens **inside / on top of** tall buildings.

3 The gardens can help keep the buildings **wet / cool**.

4 In the gardens, people can enjoy **nature / sports** in the city!

2 In pairs, plan a rooftop garden. Follow the steps below.

Step 1: What kinds of plants?

◯ fruits   ◯ vegetables   ◯ flowers   ◯ trees

Notes: ....

Step 2: Where do the plants go?

- Think about their sizes.
- How much sun do they need?
- How many do you want to plant?

Notes: ....

....

Step 3:  In your notebook, draw and label your garden.

peas   tomatoes   carrots   flowers

3 How will you take care of your rooftop garden? In pairs, talk about what you will do.

weed the garden   get bees   plant   water   add soil

 First we'll plant the seeds.

Yes, and then we'll have to water them every day.

Find Out

1   **Write one word on each line.**

> boring   classroom   microphone   screen   turn

1 Each telepresence robot has a .... and a camera.

2 Children can use a telepresence robot to see the .... from the hospital.

3 If you're not in school for a long time, it can be ....

4 When Gemma talks into the .... her classmates can hear her.

5 With its wheels, the robot can .... and move around the school.

2   💡 **In pairs, imagine you have a robot. What three things do you want it to do?**

Writing tip

> *The robot has wheels* **and** *can move around.*
> *Gemma is in hospital,* **but** *she isn't missing school.*
>
> Use *and* and *but* to join two sentences. Put a comma before *but*.

3   **How does Gemma use her robot? Write *and* or *but* and the correct punctuation.**

Gemma turns on her computer .... puts on her headphones. She can see her classroom .... she can't hear the teacher. What's wrong? She looks at the settings .... turns on the sound. That's better! The teacher asks a question .... Gemma's robot answers. "That's a good guess .... it's the wrong answer," says the teacher. "Try again."

Game Pair Quiz

Student A

1a At the beginning of the story, what does Hiro do?

2a Spell it.
Hiro heard the explosion and fell to his ....ees.

3a What does the green chip do?

4a What isn't part of a computer?
chip   disk   mind   screen

5a How can rooftop gardens help the environment? Give one example.

6a Name one part of a telepresence robot.

7a What will happen to Baymax next?

8a Make a question and ask your partner.

Student B

1b At the beginning of the story, what does Tadashi want Hiro to do?

2b Spell it.
Honey took a ....otogra .... of the masked man.

3b What does the red chip do?

4b What do you see or hear in an explosion?
smoke   mask   noise   fire

5b What spaces in big cities aren't used much?

6b How can a telepresence robot help a sick child in class? Give one example.

7b What will happen to Hiro and Abigail next?

8b Make a question and ask your partner.

Now I can ...

○ understand a story about robots and superheroes.

○ make predictions about the future using *will*.

○ read, spell, and say words with *kn* and *ph*.

Book 6

DISNEY · PIXAR
RATATOUILLE
(rat·a·too·ee)

GUSTEAU'S

What is the sign for? How does Remy feel about it? Think and talk.

Vocabulary

1 **Look and write.**

There's a lot of soup. The pot is ....

Emile's eating ....

Remy .... Linguini's hands.

.... makes food taste better.

The rats' boat is going into the ....

This is the .... for Gusteau's restaurant.

2 **Match the sentences 1–5 to the words a–e.**

1 You read it before you go to a new restaurant to see if it's good. ....

2 You can watch it on TV or read it online. ....

3 A good chef has it. A bad chef doesn't have it. ....

4 It describes what you are when you lose your job. ....

5 When you go back to a place. ....

a news

b return

c review

d talent

e fired

3 📝 **In groups, discuss how these words are related. In your notebook, write three sentences with any of these words.**

> ingredient   meal   recipe   salt   stew   delicious

You don't have to use a **recipe** to make a **stew**.

Story

1 **How did the characters feel? Choose and write.**

afraid   angry   excited   nervous   sad   surprised   unhappy

1 [2] Remy heard that Gusteau was dead. He .... *felt sad* ....

2 [4] Remy saw the sign. He ....

3 [20] Anton Ego visited the restaurant. Linguini ....

4 [24] Linguini saw the rats. He ....

2 **Complete the story arc. Write the sentence numbers.**

4 Climax ◯

3 Event ◯

5 Event ◯

2 Event ◯

1 Opening ◯

6 Resolution ◯

a Linguini becomes famous. People don't know that the real chef is Remy.

b Linguini finds the rats in the storeroom. He and Remy fight. Remy leaves.

c *Gusteau's* gets a five-star review! They are all happy!

d Remy returns. Colette and the rats help Remy cook Anton Ego's meal.

e Remy and Linguini meet at *Gusteau's*. Remy helps Linguini cook.

f Remy finds out that Gusteau left his restaurant to Linguini.

3 **Write about one event from the story arc in your notebook.**

Language

1 **Listen and read.**

💬 Language

This fish is **too salty**.	Use **too** + **adjective** when something is more than necessary.
This soup is *as good as* my dad's.	Use *as* + adjective + *as* when two things are equal.
This store has **the most expensive** cakes in town.	Use **the most** + **adjective** to compare three or more things.

2 **Write. Use adjectives with *too*, *as … as*, or *the most*.**

1 I can't drink this tea. It's <u>too hot!</u> .... `hot`

2 This is .... dish on the menu! `expensive`

3 Breakfast is .... dinner. `important`

4 This recipe is .... I can't make it. `difficult`

5 *Maria's* restaurant is .... *Pierre's*. `old`

3 **Look at the reviews and the menu. In pairs, make comparisons using *too*, *as … as*, or *the most* and adjectives from Activities 1 and 2.**

Restaurants
La Tomate (opened 2015) ★★★★★
The Blue Pot (opened 2015) ★★★
Nick's Café (opened 1992) ★★★

Menu
Lemon Chicken	$12
Vegetable Stew	$35
Fried Fish	$2

4 **Imagine it's your mom's birthday. Talk about the restaurants in your area and choose where to go to celebrate.**

Sushi Town is the most famous Japanese restaurant around here.

It's too expensive. *Oiishi* is as good as *Sushi Town*.

Phonics

1 🎧 Help Remy get to *Gusteau's*. Read and follow the words with a soft c sound as in *city*. Listen and check.

START

science — college — case — secret — coin — chef

voice — ceiling — chest — sentence — office

ocean — carpet — palace — piece — soccer — center

FINISH

2 🎧 Write the missing words with a soft c sound. Then listen and say.

I went there on _____, I went there t_____
The food's delicious, more than n_____!
The _____ty's best restaurant, I must say.
And you could r_____ there now, today!

Jump on your b_____, quick, and ride,
Then try the food and you d_____.
And tell me, look me in the f_____ —
Is this the _____ty's finest p_____?

3 🎧 Look and spell words with hard and soft c sounds. Which word is the odd one out? Listen and check.

1    **2**    **3**    **4**    **5**

Global Citizenship

1 **Answer the questions.**

1 What is a sad fact about food waste?

....

2 Why is food waste bad for the planet? ....

3 What does "think before you buy" mean? ....

4 What is the message of World Food Day? ....

2 **How do we create or reduce food waste? Sort the sentences. Then talk with your partner.**

Create food waste
◯ ◯ ◯

Reduce food waste
◯ ◯ ◯

1 Cook more food than you can eat.

2 Save leftovers for snacks.

3 Buy a lot of food every week.

4 Make a shopping list and only buy what's on it.

5 Share meals at restaurants.

6 Throw away "ugly" fruit and vegetables.

3 In small groups, think of a dinner. Then decide how you could use the leftovers to make another meal or a snack.

We chose roast chicken with vegetables. What can we do with the leftover chicken?

How about a chicken pie? We can use some of the leftover carrots in it, too.

Find Out

1 Complete the chart.

What is your favorite meal?
How is it similar to or different than ratatouille?

	Ratatouille
Ingredients:	Ingredients:

2 In pairs, compare your meals from Activity 1. How can you make them more interesting?

> ### Writing tip
>
> *Chop the vegetables and put them in the pan.*
> *Fry the sausages in a little oil, or grill them.*
>
> Use *and* or *or* to join two sentences. Add a comma before *or*.

3 Write *and* or *or* and the correct punctuation.

1 Keep your leftover vegetables .... make this amazing stew.

2 You can cook ratatouille in a pan .... bake all ingredients in the oven.

3 Wash the vegetables .... chop them into small pieces.

4 Put the vegetable pieces in the pan .... cook for five minutes.

5 You can serve ratatouille as a main dish .... mix it with cooked pasta.

Game Connect Four in a Line

1 What words can describe food?

- salty
- nervous
- delicious
- wonderful

2 Spell it.

There are vegetables and spi ___ ___ s in this re ___ ___ ___ ___ .

3 Make a sentence. Use the superlative form.

These are ___ cakes! (delicious)

4 Choose two places you often find rats.

- in a car
- in the sewer
- in the garbage
- in a pot

5

What do you put in ratatouille? Say three things.

6 Who doesn't cook in the story?

- Remy
- Linguini
- Anton Ego
- Colette

7 Join the sentences. Use *and* or *or*.

Beat the eggs in a bowl. Add a little milk.

8 Match the words. Use two to make a sentence.

waste	newspaper
review	customer
waiter	garbage

9 Spell it.

My scien___ ___ teacher rides her bi___ ___ cle twi___ ___ a week.

10 Join the sentences. Use *and* or *or*.

We can cook dinner at home. We can eat out at a nice restaurant.

11

What is happening in this picture? Why is the chef doing this?

12 Make sentences.

recipe / difficult / this / too / is

your / dish / as / mine / big / is / as / not

13 How can we reduce food waste? Give two examples.

14 What country does ratatouille come from?

15 Make a sentence. Use *too*.

This soup ___ ! (salty)

16 Who wrote this? What does it mean?

"A good artist can come from anywhere."

Now I can ...

○ understand a story about a rat's dream of becoming a chef.

○ compare and describe things using adjectives.

○ read, spell, and say words with a soft c sound.

1 Aa **Read, choose, and write.**

> crashed   antique   figure   kids   worry

1 The girl made a _____ out of a plastic fork and called it "Forky".

2 You can buy expensive old things at an _____ store.

3 The motorbike _____ into the tree but the man was okay.

4 Many children _____ about their first day of school.

5 The _____ played in the park all day.

2 📖 **Read and match the sentences (1–4) to the main ideas (a–d).**

1 It was difficult, but Woody looked after Forky for Bonnie. _____

2 Gabby Gabby was sad but then she found her kid. _____

3 The other toys wanted a kid, but Bo wanted to be free. _____

4 Woody went with Bo. They started a new life. _____

a It can be good to change.

b Sometimes you have to do things for others.

c Don't lose hope. Good things happen.

d Everyone is different and that's okay.

3 💬 **Put the verb in the present progressive (*I'm playing*) or the present simple (*I play*).**

1 Jake: We _____ (play) football tomorrow. Do you want to come?

2 Neela: I always _____ (practice) the piano on Saturday. So I can't come.

3 Jake: Okay. What about Sunday? I _____ (go) to the beach.

4 Neela: Sorry. We _____ (have) a big family lunch every Sunday.

1 🅰🅰 Read and match. Write the words.

swords   armor   caterpillar   disappear   battle   whisper

1 Soldiers wear these metal clothes in a battle. ....

2 In this big fight, one country or side attacks another. ....

3 This creature becomes a butterfly. ....

4 Soldiers use these long sharp pieces of metal in battles. ....

5 When people speak softly in your ear, they do this. ....

6 Rabbits do this when they go down rabbit holes. ....

2 📖 Write sentences to describe the Mad Hatter.

1 His clothes are ....

2 His hair is ....

3 His face is ....

3 💬 Write sentences. Use *could* and the words in brackets.

1 I can't open the door. I don't have the key.
   Request: .... (have)

2 I can't find my pencil.
   Suggestion: .... (borrow)

3 I'm thirsty.
   Request: .... (have / water)

4 I forgot my lunchbox.
   Suggestion: .... (buy / food)

1 🅰️🅰️ **Read and circle.**

1 The captain was not afraid. He fought **bravely / quietly** and won!

2 The hospital was full of **broken / angry** robots.

3 The machine scanned the bag, and the **alarm / detector** started. It was very loud.

4 The big robots picked up the trash and **squashed / exploded** it into cubes.

5 The girl was nervous and very **sick / shy**. She hid behind her mom.

2 📖 **Read sentences 1–3 and match to sentences a–c.**

1 WALL-E wanted to hold hands and dance like the people in the movie. ....

2 He moved to hide behind another rock, but he made a noise. ....

3 Earth didn't look so ugly from space. ....

a WALL-E was lonely.

b WALL-E was scared.

c Earth looked ugly on the ground.

3 💬 **Choose and write.**

anything   everywhere   nothing   something

1 The boy wanted a friend more than ....

2 The boy stopped. He heard .... It was an alarm.

3 The children looked .... for their toy robot. They couldn't find it.

4 I pushed all the buttons, but .... worked. The computer didn't start.

1 🅰️ **Label the pictures.**

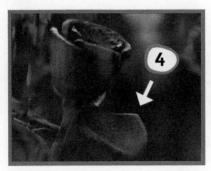

1 _____   3 _____   5 _____

2 _____   4 _____

2 📖 **Compare Gaston and the Beast. Write two similarities and two differences. Use these words.**

> alone   angry   kind   many friends   marry Belle   strong   unkind

Similarities

1 Both are _____ and _____.

2 Both want to _____.

Differences

3 Gaston is _____, but the Beast becomes _____ at the end of the story.

4 The Beast is usually _____, but Gaston has _____.

3 💬 **Match 1–5 to a–e to make sentences.**

1 If I like a story, ...   a I don't read it.

2 If a story is boring, ...   b I don't read it at bedtime.

3 If you read a story out loud, ...   c I have to read it slowly.

4 If a story is scary, ...   d I read it again and again.

5 If a story is in English, ...   e you remember it better.

1 Aa Read and match. Write the words.

> video   chip   portal   explosion   lab   machine

1 This is a real or imagined door to something. ....

2 There is usually a loud noise, smoke and fire when this happens. ....

3 This is where scientists work. ....

4 Engineers build this to do jobs more quickly. ....

5 This can be a movie or a television program. ....

6 If you put this small thing into a robot, it can help program it. ....

2 Read and answer the questions.

1 What happened when Hiro was three? ....

2 Who did Tadashi and Hiro live with? ....

3 What kind of robot is Baymax? ....

4 What did Hiro make for the student show? ....

5 Why was Callaghan angry with Krei? ....

3 What will happen in 2035? Write sentences using *will* + verb.

1 What will computers look like? ....

2 How big will cell phones be? ....

3 Will people live in space? ....

4 How old will you be? ....

5 Will you drive a car? ....

1 🅰️ **Read, choose, and circle.**

The new chef wanted to make a **show / stew / pot.** There was a good **recipe / review / meal** in a book. He opened the cupboard with his **foot / key / spoon** and found the cookbook. He took some potatoes, carrots and meat, and put all the **forks / secrets / ingredients** into a pot. Then he put some **sign / salt / garbage** into the pot. Oh no! It all fell into the pot! He tasted the stew. Yuck! It wasn't **funny / full / delicious.** He threw it into the **sewer / fridge / garbage** can.

2 📖 **How do the <u>underlined</u> characters feel? Match.**

1 The <u>rats</u> ran away from the woman. ....   **a afraid**

2 "Where is the soup?" shouted <u>Chef Skinner</u>. ....   **b nervous**

3 "Remy! You're alive!" said <u>Emile</u>. ....   **c angry**

4 Linguini wasn't really the chef. <u>Remy</u> was. ....   **d happy**

5 The other chefs arrived, and <u>Linguini</u> had to cook without Remy. ....   **e sad**

3 💬 **The underlined words are in the wrong sentences. Write them in the correct places.**

1 Ouch! This soup is <u>**as bad as**</u> ....!

2 Yum! These cookies are <u>**the biggest**</u> .... my mom's cookies.

3 This is <u>**too cold**</u> .... restaurant in the city.

4 Yuck The stew is <u>**the best**</u> .... Put it back in the oven.

5 Oh no! This pizza is <u>**as delicious as**</u> .... the last one.

6 It's huge! My dad bought <u>**too hot**</u> .... cake in the bakery!

Reading Record

Book 1
Toy Story 4

My rating: ☆☆☆☆☆

This book:

My new words:

STAMP

Book 2
Alice in Wonderland

My rating: ☆☆☆☆☆

This book:

My new words:

STAMP

Book 3
WALL-E

My rating: ☆☆☆☆☆

This book:

My new words:

STAMP

Book 4
Beauty and the Beast

My rating: ☆☆☆☆☆

This book:

My new words:

STAMP

Book 5
Big Hero 6

My rating: ☆☆☆☆☆

This book:

My new words:

STAMP

Book 6
Ratatouille

My rating: ☆☆☆☆☆

This book:

My new words:

STAMP

Spelling Practice

Common words	Look and write.	Cover and write.		✔
will				
won't				
another				
each				
first				
last				
then				
finally				
suddenly				
soon				
once				
twice				
again				
piece				
little				
something				
nothing				
everywhere				
anywhere				
yesterday				
tomorrow				
past				
future				
same				
different				
favorite				
million				
billion				

Irregular past tense verbs	Look. Write the second word.	Cover and write.		✔
read → read				
make → made				
come → came				
leave → left				
take → took				
give → gave				
feel → felt				
meet → met				
keep → kept				
build → built				
find → found				
drive → drove				
sit → sat				
stand → stood				
fall → fell				
break → broke				
begin → began				
swim → swam				
buy → bought				
fight → fought				
think → thought				
catch → caught				
throw → threw				
draw → drew				
fly → flew				
know → knew				
grow → grew				

Word List

a

actor
agree
alarm
alive
along
already
another
antique
anything
anywhere
appear
armor
as ... as
as soon as
astronaut
at first
at last
attack

b

backpack
battle
beast
believe
bell pepper
bicycle
billion
boy
brave

break a spell
breathe
bridge
broken
brother
brown
butter
button

c

camp
candlestick
carnival
carousel
caterpillar
ceiling
center
century
champion
change
character
chef
chest
chip
chop
chute
city
class
classmate
coin
college

color
control
court
crash
crayon
crazy
create
creature
critic
customer
cut off

d

danger
dead
dear
decide
deck
decompose
delicious
dentist
destroy
detector
disappear
dish
disk
doorknob
down
down with
during

e

each
Earth
eggplant
elephant
empty
enchantress
energy
enough
eraser
escape
ever
every
everything
everywhere
exercise
explain
explode
explosion
eyebrow

f

fact
factory
fairy tale
far
female
figure
fire extinguisher
fired

forehead
fresh
fridge
friendly
frighten
full

g

garbage
garlic
glue
GPS

h

habit
headphones
healthy
height
herbs
hole
horrible
house
huge
human

i

if
intelligent
ingredient
inspire

j

jar
join
Jupiter
just

k

key
kid
kindergarten
kiss
knee
knife
knit
knock
knot

l

lab
lamp
land
large
later
law
leftovers
let
letter
like
live happily
ever after
lock

look
look after
look like
lost

m

machine
made of
magic
makeup
marry
mask
maybe
meal
metal
microphone
microplastics
million
mind
mirror
miss
motorbike
mouth

n

nature
need
nervous
news
newspaper
none
nothing
nurse

o

off with
office
oil
once
onion
organization
other
owl
owner

p

palace
pan
pepper
petal
phone
photo
piece
pilot
pin
planet
plastic
pod
point
popular
portal
pot
prince
program
promise
put a spell on

q

queen

r

rabbit
race
rat
real
recipe
recognize
reduce
return
review
rocket
roar
robot
rose
RV

s

safe
salt
scan
science
screen
second
secret
sentence
sewer
sheep
shoot
shoulder

show
shy
sick
side
sign
since
single
smoke
so
soccer
soldier
someone
something
somewhere
soon
soup
space pod
speaker
spell
spice
squash
staff
steal
step
stew
still
stone
storeroom
strange
string
student
supper

sure
survive
sweater
sword

t

tablet
take off
take power
talent
tape
tavern
teapot
teenager
telepresence
theater
tie
toe
together
toilet
too
toward
tower
towel
town
toy
trash
travel
trophy
turn off
turn on
twice

u

until

v

vegan
Venus
video
visitor
voice

w

waiter
waste
water
when
whisper
whole
wig
will
winter
wolf
work
worried

y

yet

z

zero
zucchini

Pearson English Kids Readers

Read and learn with Disney friends!

Disney Kids Readers bring to life the magic of Disney stories in carefully graded English. They motivate learners to read in and out of the classroom, encouraging a lifelong love of reading.

Disney Kids Readers course is built on five key principles:

- Rich, memorable stories with relatable characters make reading a pleasure

- Careful grading, reading support, and gentle but visible progression give a sense of achievement

- Building literacy skills alongside language skills deepens understanding of fiction, and helps young learners to express thoughts and feelings

- Built on the Global Scale of English: rigorous pedagogical foundations and support materials

- Easy and flexible to teach, with step-by-step lesson plans

Course components by Level

- 6 Readers
- 6 Audiobooks
- 6 Teacher's Notes and Photocopiables
- Workbook and eBook
- Teacher's Book

LEVEL	CEFR	GSE	CYLETS	PTE YL
1	<A1-A1	16-27	Starters	Firstwords
2	A1-A2	22-32	Starters/Movers	Firstwords/Springboard
3	A1-A2	25-35	Movers	Springboard
4	A1-A2+	27-38	Movers	Springboard/Quickmarch
5	A2-A2+	30-40	Movers/Flyers	Quickmarch/Breakthrough
6	A2+-B1	36-48	Flyers	Breakthrough

ISBN 978-1-292-33084-6

TEAM Together

Top Tips and Practice
for PTE Young Learners

QUICKMARCH & BREAKTHROUGH

Sarah Gudgeon

Your course comes with extra digital resources on the **Pearson English Portal**.

To access the Portal:

1   Go to **english.com/activate**

2   Sign in or create an account

3   Enter the access code below and click **activate**

This code can only be used once and the user subscription is valid for 24 months from the date of registration.

Need help?

Go to **english.com/help** for support with:

- Creating your account
- Activating your access code
- Checking technical requirements
- Using apps